CLIMATE
REBELS

BEN LERWILL

PUFFIN

*We live on an utterly extraordinary planet.
It is big, beautiful and bursting
with magical natural gifts.*

It is a world of dazzling sunsets, deep oceans, snow-topped mountains and teeming jungles . . . but it's in trouble. Our home deserves our protection, and right now it needs every act of care we can give it. This book tells the stories of ordinary people who have been inspired to stand up and make a real difference to the future of our world. These stories bring us hope, but they also show us something vital: that no matter where we live, or how old we are, we too can make a difference.

'THE GREATEST
THREAT TO OUR PLANET
IS THE BELIEF
THAT SOMEONE ELSE
WILL SAVE IT.'

- ROBERT SWAN, OBE

CONTENTS

INTRODUCTION:
AN INTERVIEW WITH DR JANE GOODALL

When did you realize your conservation work was making a real, positive difference?

I was invited to speak at a meeting of international tropical hardwood timber companies around 1990. I did not want to meet these people who were destroying the forests I loved, but I went. I talked about my relationship with the forests, the harm that the big corporations were causing in Africa. I told them about the lives of the chimpanzees and how these were disrupted. I told stories. I explained how the roads they made enabled hunters to go deeper and deeper into the forests. At the end many people came up for me to sign copies of my books. One CEO of a very big American company was crying. He could not speak but hurried away.

Afterwards he wrote. Would I attend a very private meeting of the CEOs of the five or six largest companies in Switzerland? One of the men was responsible for writing the code of conduct that stipulated what size a tree must be before it could be harvested, how far apart they must be, how many years before that section of the forest could be logged again. And after that meeting, he wrote to tell me that he had added a code of conduct which stipulated that there should be no logging in chimpanzee habitats. I was amazed.

What drives you to keep campaigning for an environment that betters the lives of all living things?

I have loved animals and nature since I was a child. I have travelled the world and seen the destruction wrought by my own species. The once great forest that stretched across Africa is now a series of gradually decreasing fragments. Gombe National Park was once part of that forest – by 1980 it was an isolated island of trees. The chimpanzees are gone from some of their former range and are endangered in others. More and more animal and plant species are becoming extinct.

But I believe there is still a window of time when, if we all get together, we can start to heal the hurt we have inflicted on mother nature, and at least slow down climate change. I am often told that my lectures give people some hope, so I have to keep on doing what I can for the sake of the natural world that I love, and for future generations. At eighty-five years old I cannot slow down – but must speed up to make the most of the years I have left.

Why do you believe it is so vital to engage and inform young people?

There is a saying: 'We haven't inherited the world from our parents, we've borrowed it from our children'. But we have not borrowed, we've *stolen* their future and we are still stealing.

Adults are often set in their ways. Children are flexible and they can influence their parents and grandparents. Once they understand the problems and are empowered to take action, they show so much determination and energy. In 1991, when I realized that so many young people were losing hope or were simply apathetic, I decided to start our Roots & Shoots programme with twelve Tanzanian high-school children. Its main message: every individual matters, every individual has a role to play, and every individual makes an impact on the planet – EVERY DAY. Today, in some sixty countries, it has members in kindergartens, universities and everything in between. Each group chooses three projects: to help people; to help animals; to help the environment. Choices vary according to individual passions, nationality, religion, culture, age and wealth. Roots & Shoots, and other youth groups with a similar philosophy, are changing the world even as you read this.

We're living in an era that can feel frightening. Do you see reasons to feel optimistic about the future?

My greatest reason for hope is our young people.

Secondly, there is our amazing intellect. Animals are WAY more intelligent than people used to think, but even the brightest chimp or dolphin or crow cannot compare to some human technological achievements. Every time I look at the moon, I think with awe of how human beings have been able to walk there – wow! And now we have clean green energy, we have ways of sucking CO_2 out of the atmosphere, and incredible new technologies are in the pipeline.

But we must, at the same time, each make our own efforts to minimize our ecological footprints. Make ethical choices in what we buy, eat and wear. Reduce global consumption of meat and eliminate poverty, for the really poor cannot afford to make ethical choices. They must clear the last trees to grow food or make charcoal in their desperate efforts to feed themselves and their family. And in urban areas they must buy the cheapest junk food to simply stay alive.

The next reason for hope is the resilience of nature. Given time, and perhaps some help, places we destroyed can once again become beautiful. The natural world could return. First the plants, followed by animals.

Finally, there is the indomitable human spirit: those who tackle what seems impossible and won't give up. I have written books about my reasons for hope, and I believe that we must make changes, but we do still have reason to hope.

Dr Jane Goodall, DBE
Founder of the Jane Goodall Institute & UN Messenger of Peace
To find out more about Jane's work visit: *www.janegoodall.org.uk*
www.rootsnshoots.org.uk

DR JANE GOODALL

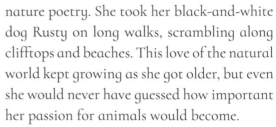

The year was 1960. In the middle of a hot, tropical jungle, Jane Goodall held out a banana to a chimpanzee. She was in East Africa, in what is now Tanzania, working in a place so wild and remote that it could only be reached by boat. For months she had been trying to learn about the chimpanzees here, but they were nervous around humans and would swing away through the trees. Not today. The chimpanzee looked at the banana, edged towards Jane and took it from her hand. Jane's heart leaped. At last – at last! – these wonderful creatures were starting to trust her.

Some people are born to care for animals. When Jane was one-and-a-half years old, growing up in England, she gathered a big handful of wriggly worms from her garden and took them up to her bed. You might think this was an odd thing to do – and certainly Jane's mother thought so. She explained to her daughter that worms needed soil, not bedclothes, to survive. So the little girl hurriedly took them back down to the garden where they belonged.

Jane was besotted with wildlife in other ways too. She liked to sit watching hedgehogs and squirrels. She wrote nature poetry. She took her black-and-white dog Rusty on long walks, scrambling along clifftops and beaches. This love of the natural world kept growing as she got older, but even she would never have guessed how important her passion for animals would become.

Jane was twenty-six when she began working in Gombe, western Tanzania (in what is today Gombe National Park). At this time people had very little information about how chimpanzees lived – in fact, almost nothing was known about their behaviour in the wild. Jane wanted to change that. Some scientists thought it was ridiculous to be sending a young woman into the jungle alone. Jane didn't agree. She was glad to make the green, sweaty tangle of the trees her office.

Through months and years of patient study, Jane opened the world's eyes to how amazing and intelligent chimpanzees can be. No creature on Earth has more in common with humans, and Jane helped us

AT LAST — AT LAST! —
THESE WONDERFUL
CREATURES WERE
STARTING TO
TRUST HER

to appreciate this. She saw that they used long pieces of grass to 'fish' for insects in termite nests. She saw that mothers and babies had close, powerful bonds, just like humans do. And she saw that chimpanzees fought, and sometimes even hurt each other.

She also learned – thanks to her favourite chimpanzee, whom she named David Greybeard, after the white hairs on his chin – that they were able to show trust and kindness, not just to each other but to people too. It was David Greybeard who had taken that first banana from her hand. And, when he died of an illness in 1968, Jane became even more determined to do everything she could to understand and protect chimpanzees.

Her work has never stopped. In 1977 she founded the Jane Goodall Institute, which researches the lives of wild chimpanzees, the welfare of captive chimpanzees, and works with local communities. It also works with young

people around the world through its Roots & Shoots programme. Jane also campaigns for the people who live in, and around, our forests, and who know them best – as well as the animals that live there.

Decades after her first trip to the jungle, Jane is still inspiring us to love and value wild creatures. She spends around 300 days a year travelling the world to spread her message. There are fewer than 300,000 chimpanzees left in the wild anywhere – and Jane is determined to help this number to rise.

SIR DAVID ATTENBOROUGH

Polar bears padding through an Arctic snowstorm. Sharks swimming silently on the Great Barrier Reef. Gorillas crashing through the Rwandan jungle. If you've ever watched a wildlife documentary, there's a very good chance that one man's voice was telling you, clearly but quietly, all about what you were looking at. Sir David Attenborough is a man whose name will be remembered for many decades to come, not only for his incredible TV programmes but also for his work in helping to make a greener, cleaner world.

His fame came by accident. In September 1954, as a nature-loving twenty-eight-year-old TV producer, he made his first trip outside Europe, travelling to Sierra Leone in Africa to help film scenes for a new programme called *Zoo Quest*. He arrived into a heat and humidity he had never known before. Within minutes he had spotted sunbirds flitting between red hibiscus flowers and a chameleon slinking along a branch. He was hooked.

However, when he and the team got back to England with their film footage, there was a problem. David's friend Jack Lester, who was supposed to be presenting *Zoo Quest*, had been taken ill. A replacement needed to be found, so David agreed to step in front of the cameras and take Jack's place. His warm manner and enthusiasm made him popular straight away. Before long he was a familiar face on the television.

Since that day David has travelled to almost every corner of the globe, sharing the wonders of the planet with hundreds of millions of viewers. His programmes have taken us into the lives of people on remote islands, shown us the miracles of tropical plants and explained to us the magic and mystery of the animal kingdom. For more than half a century David has shown the world to the world.

But that's not all. Over the decades, some of the dangers facing the Earth have become far more serious, and David has tried to ensure that these dangers are not ignored. He wrote and presented a three-part series called *State of the Planet*, which was shown on television in 2000. It taught viewers about everything from pollution to habitat loss. In 2007 he also helped with a series called *Saving Planet Earth*, which

showed us the importance of wildlife conservation.

More recently, his *Blue Planet II* series has made people more aware of the deadly amount of plastic in the oceans. When viewers saw how big the problem was, they were shocked and saddened. It has made many of us much more careful about using plastic. The series had such a big impact across the world that experts now talk about 'the Blue Planet effect', which has helped to change how we think about plastic.

David has led a truly extraordinary life. He was knighted by the Queen all the way back in 1985. For some people, receiving an honour like that might make them slow down and work less hard. But not David. Since then he has been to some of the hottest, coldest, wildest and most

remote spots in the world, always explaining to us why these places are so special. And he's still a passionate supporter of many different charities, including the World Land Trust, which helps to keep wildlife safe by looking after our rainforests.

His influence on the world has been so huge that there are even species of plants and animals named after him. In the jungles of South America lives a very rare butterfly with delicate striped wings and pretty spots. Its name is *Euptychia attenboroughi*, or Attenborough's black-eyed satyr. This precious insect, fluttering quietly through the green depths of the Amazon rainforest, carries the name of a man who has been a true champion of the natural world.

THE FOUNDERS OF GREENPEACE

In the autumn of 1971 an old fishing boat set sail across the Gulf of Alaska. The boat was in need of repairs and the captain was missing most of his teeth, but the twelve people on board were on a mission. The American government planned to test nuclear weapons on an Alaskan island. The twelve people were sailing to the island to try and stop them. Why? Because this test would put wildlife in danger and possibly even cause an earthquake. And from this voyage – with a battered boat struggling through the waves to stand up to a powerful government – a very special organization was born.

Greenpeace is the largest environmental movement in the world. It has offices on six continents and almost three million supporters across the globe. Its aim is to

protect our planet: our trees, our air, our seas, our wildlife. But, like many large organizations, it began its life as something quite small. In fact, if it hadn't been for a handful of very committed activists, it might never have existed at all.

When this small group of Canadians and Americans decided to hire a boat and sail to Alaska to try and halt the tests, they didn't realize how much impact their idea would have. The group – which included Irving and Dorothy Stowe, Jim and Marie Bohlen and Paul Côté – christened the boat *Greenpeace*, a name that summed up the cause they were fighting for. And when the story of the boat's voyage appeared in the news, they saw they could make a real difference.

Soon Greenpeace was more than just a boat. It was a movement determined to prevent world leaders and big businesses from doing risky and selfish things. It fought to protect whales and seals. It campaigned to stop other countries making unsafe nuclear tests. Through

non-violent action, it tried to make life as difficult as possible for anyone harming the environment. And very often it succeeded!

By the 1980s, Greenpeace had many thousands of supporters and a whole fleet of boats. The people who worked for the organization learned that, with the right sort of protest, their message could be heard by millions of people. They forced chemical companies to stop dumping waste in the sea. They became a thorn in the side of governments harming the environment. And when their most famous boat, the *Rainbow Warrior*, was sunk by the French secret service in 1985, it made them even more determined to keep fighting.

In the years since then, Greenpeace has grown and grown. It has always spoken up for our planet and its wildlife, campaigning for change everywhere from Antarctica to the Amazon rainforest. It has put pressure on fast-food chains, fashion brands and car makers to be environmentally friendly. And more than anything, Greenpeace has never been afraid to stand up for what it feels is right.

Many of its protests have been unforgettable. Some Greenpeace activists have climbed high statues, towers or oil rigs to fly flags and banners, while others have used costumes to get their point across. In Moscow they've worn polar bear outfits to campaign against drilling in the Arctic, in China they've dressed as orangutans to stop the use of palm oil, and in the Philippines they've marched through the streets in zombie make-up to protest against toxic waste!

Today, Greenpeace is still making its voice heard around the world. Many laws have been improved because of the work it has done for the planet. But without that first brave group of activists in the early 1970s who saw something unfair and decided to act, there would be no story to write about here. Those activists realized something very important: that by refusing to ignore the environmental damage that was going on, they could make change happen.

MANY OF ITS PROTESTS HAVE BEEN UNFORGETTABLE

MARINEL UBALDO

On the day the typhoon arrived, 13 November 2013, the fishing village didn't stand a chance. Fierce storms thundered in from the sea, tearing the trees out of the earth and blowing the roofs from the houses. The wind howled, the rain poured, the skies raged. In the middle of it all, one teenager watched in horror as the buildings around her splintered and collapsed.

Marinel Ubaldo was just sixteen when Super Typhoon Yolanda (also known as Typhoon Haiyan) smashed into her coastal village, Matarinao, in the Philippines. Local people had been told a storm was on the way, but no one had realized just how strong it would be. For days after the typhoon, the shocked villagers were left stranded with no fresh food, electricity, water, shelter or dry clothes. Tragically, eleven of them lost their lives.

For a long time afterwards, Marinel was traumatized. She became terrified of the wind and rain. The storms had destroyed her house and the floods had carried away almost everything she owned. One very precious item was lost forever: a box in which she had kept all the things she was proudest of, like her school medals and certificates. Losing this box made Marinel feel as though she had lost the person she used to be. To make matters worse, the storm had wrecked her father's fishing boat, which made it difficult for the family to survive.

But she didn't want to be seen as a victim. Instead, she wanted to help prevent disasters like this. Storms are not unusual in the Philippines, but Super Typhoon Yolanda was one of the fiercest tropical cyclones of all time. Marinel knew that climate change was making these extreme weather events more likely, so she focused on spreading this message to as many people as possible – through local meetings, radio interviews and even street theatre. Today, she still makes headlines by campaigning against big companies that are harming the environment.

Marinel wants to be able to tell the next generation that she fought not only for her own future, but for theirs too. She wants young people everywhere to know that the impact of climate change is already being felt – and that everyone has the power to make a difference.

RACHEL CARSON

A good book can be a powerful thing. It seems strange that an object small enough to slip into your school bag is able to change the way the world thinks, but it's true. The words on a page can make a difference to the actions of millions of people, and this is the case with one very special book. Even now, almost sixty years after it was published, it remains influential. Its name is *Silent Spring*.

Its author, Rachel Carson, was born in Pennsylvania in the USA, in 1907. From an early age she had a deep love of nature. She explored the rivers and wetlands near her home and made up stories about wild birds and rabbits. As she grew older she developed a special fascination with the ocean, and after studying hard she became an aquatic biologist – an expert in sea life.

Rachel wrote three books about the wonders of the ocean, taking her readers from the silvery waves to the deep dark seabeds, but it was her fourth book, *Silent Spring*, that made the world sit up and take notice.

It was about the danger of pesticides, which are chemicals often sprayed on to crops – usually by planes or farm vehicles – to kill plants or animals that are harmful to farm produce. But it was also about much more than that. It reminded us how the things we humans do can cause serious damage to nature. The book's title came from Rachel imagining a future when – because of the effects of pesticides – there would be no birds left to sing in the springtime.

Silent Spring made some pesticide companies very angry, but it became a bestseller. These days we remember it as one of the first books to shape how we think about the environment. Rachel died suddenly when she was just fifty-six years old. Written by an extraordinary woman who saw things in an extraordinary way, her book inspired countless people to campaign against pollution. And, more than anything, it still inspires us to stand up and make ourselves heard.

JOHN MUIR

More than 170 years ago, in the Scottish seaside town of Dunbar, a young schoolboy used to walk along the coastline looking at the flowers, the insects and the waves. But he was more than a dreamer. He would grow up to be a man who travelled the globe, met presidents and changed the way the world looks after its wild places.

John Muir was born in 1838. When he was ten years old, he and his family emigrated from Scotland to the USA, sailing across the Atlantic Ocean to start a new life. The family settled on a farm, where John – who had no school to go to – taught himself maths, literature and other subjects. He got up in the middle of the night to read and learn.

However, his real passion was the outdoors. After nearly going blind in an accident when he was twenty-eight, he decided to undertake an amazing 1,000-mile walk to admire the plants, woods and plains of the USA. Still wanting to see more, he later visited California, where the beauty of the mountains astonished him. He climbed summits, hiked for days and wrote articles about the glory of the American outdoors.

John also saw how important it was for these places to be protected. He set up one of the first environmental groups in the world, the Sierra Club, and tried to persuade the government to look after the countryside. In 1903, he took President Theodore Roosevelt on a camping trip to Yosemite in California. Surrounded by its towering cliffs and tumbling waterfalls, John explained to the president how vital it was that areas like this were kept special.

It worked. The president helped to create national parks, national forests and nature reserves all across the USA. But John's work was not finished. He showed Yosemite to the next president too, and spent the rest of his life campaigning for the conservation of wildernesses. That small boy who once walked the Scottish coastline, marvelling at what was around him, helped to create a national parks movement that spread across the world. He also recognized something which is still true today: that the best way for people to fall in love with the outdoors, and to seek to protect it, is for them to experience it themselves.

THE BEAUTY OF
THE MOUNTAINS
ASTONISHED HIM

ANDREW TURTON & PETE CEGLINSKI

Have you ever had a brilliant idea for an invention, then realized how tricky it would be to make? That's what happened to an Australian man called Andrew Turton, who kept noticing plastic bottles in the ocean when he was sailing. He came up with a plan to put rubbish bins in the sea to collect all the litter. It was a fantastic idea, but for a long time he wasn't quite sure how to make it happen. In fact, if it hadn't been for Pete Ceglinski, the idea might still be floating around, waiting to become a reality.

Andrew and Pete both grew up on the east coast of Australia. They swam and surfed whenever they could, riding the waves and developing a love of the ocean. Because of his surname, Andrew's nickname was Turtle! But although the two grew up in the same country, doing lots of the same things, they didn't meet until later in life, when they were both working as boat-builders for yacht-racing teams.

Their jobs meant they had to travel the world, moving from continent to continent. Wherever they went, however, they noticed one thing remained the same. The harbours and marinas that they visited were always full of bobbing bottles, cigarette ends and other floating rubbish. They saw how this was not only polluting our water worldwide, but also causing real harm to marine life like dolphins, seals and sea turtles. Surely, they thought, there must be a way of solving the problem. That's when Andrew told Pete about the idea he'd had a few years earlier, to make a bin that would sit in the water and gather litter. His friend's eyes lit up.

Pete had been a product designer before becoming a boat-builder, and he was excited by Andrew's idea. The even better news was that he thought he could find a way of making it work. He started designing how the bin might look and how it might catch rubbish. The next step was to try and build one. Pete didn't have any money to help him, so to make the first bin he taught himself how to join metal together, how to sew and how to work with electrics.

The bin he created was a large ring that floated on the surface of the water, with a 'catch bag' dangling underneath it.

THE HARBOURS AND MARINAS ALWAYS HAD BOBBING BOTTLES, CIGARETTE ENDS AND OTHER FLOATING RUBBISH

To Pete's delight, it did exactly what it was supposed to do. It was able to suck in bottles and other bits of rubbish from the sea around it, trapping all the litter in the bag. Just as importantly, because the ring floated so high in the water, there was very little danger of fish or other sea creatures being caught inside. The invention was given a name – the Seabin – and by 2017 it was ready to be used worldwide.

Fast-forward to today and there are hundreds of Seabins catching rubbish in more than forty-five different countries. Every single piece of litter in the sea is part of a growing global problem. There are now many more pieces of plastic in the ocean than there are people in the world. Trying to fight this, each Seabin is able to collect 90,000 plastic bags or 50,000 plastic water bottles every year. They pull in crisp packets, coffee cups and even surface oil. They're cheap to run and simple to empty. The waves in the middle of the ocean make it too difficult for Seabins to work properly there, so they're used in ports and marinas instead, but the difference they make is huge. In the first two years the bins have collected more than 400 tons of rubbish. That's the same weight as 800 fully grown bottlenose dolphins!

Pete and the Seabin team are working to increase the number of Seabins worldwide. They also work with local communities and children to take better care of their rubbish in the first place. The time and effort that Pete and Andrew put into creating a floating rubbish bin has been worth it – but their real dream is that there might be a time when there's no more rubbish left to collect, and the wonderful creatures that live in our oceans can have the seas to themselves again.

JIA WENQI & JIA HAIXIA

Trees are the lungs of the world. By absorbing carbon dioxide and releasing oxygen, they help make our air breathable, and our planet liveable. Without them – without the trillions of trunks that spear into the sky from our forests, parks and gardens – the planet would be in serious trouble. Trees are our future, and two extraordinary men in rural China understood this very clearly. They also understood that, when people work together, nothing is impossible.

Jia Wenqi and Jia Haixia did not have easy childhoods. Wenqi had a terrible accident when he was just three years old, losing both his arms after touching a dangerous electric cable. Haixia, meanwhile, was born blind in one eye. The two were friends as children, but it wasn't until many years later, when Haixia lost the sight in his other eye, that they became a team.

Growing up, Wenqi had learned how to do amazing things with his feet. Using his toes, he could write, carry buckets of water and even chop vegetables. With no arms, however, it was very hard for him to find work. So when Haixia became depressed after going blind, Wenqi had an idea. 'You be my arms,' he said to his friend, 'and I'll be your eyes.'

It was 2002. The two men were in their early forties, and they were determined to spend their days doing something positive. The countryside around them had grown bare and grey since their schooldays – they remembered birds in the sky, rabbits in the hills and fish in the rivers. So they decided to plant trees. They wanted to help bring the countryside back to life – and with this thought spurring them on, they got to work.

The two men made an unusual pair, walking into the fields every day with Haixia holding on to Wenqi's empty jacket sleeve to guide him. If they had to cross a river, Wenqi would carry Haixia on his back. They had no money for seeds or saplings, so they worked together to cut small branches from other trees, which they then planted upright. To find these

TWO FRIENDS,

WORKING TOGETHER,

PLANTING A FOREST

FOR THE FUTURE

branches, Wenqi used his shoulders to help Haixia climb up into the trees, then told his blind friend where to place his arms and legs, and where to cut. Once they had small branches to plant, Wenqi used his toes to position them over holes in the earth, then Haixia pushed them into the soil.

By the end of their first year, the men had planted 800 trees. But when they went back in the spring to check on them – disaster! Only two of the trees were still alive. The soil was too dry for them to survive. Many people would have given up after this, but not Wenqi and Haixia. They realized that for the trees to thrive, they needed to be close to water. So they tried again, this time planting trees near the river. Before long, the trees started growing.

Over the next ten years, the two men planted more than 10,000 trees together. They took an island in the middle of the river and turned it into a small forest. This so impressed the person in charge of their village that he gave them more land in the nearby hills. In 2016, their story became famous, and soon people around the world were being inspired by their teamwork and single-mindedness.

Since that time, Wenqi and Haixia have both continued planting trees, sometimes together, sometimes with the help of other people. 'If everyone planted one or two trees a year,' Wenqi once said, 'imagine the difference we could make.' Their tale is a remarkable one, but at its heart is a very simple idea: two friends, working together, planting a forest for the future.

THE GUAJAJARA GUARDIANS

When you walk through the Amazon rainforest, the wilderness swallows you up. The trees are thick and hung with creepers. The rivers are slow and crawling with life. The monkeys are loud, the snakes are stealthy and the birds are dressed in bright feathers. Everywhere is noise, heat and greenery. The Amazon is one of the wonders of the planet, an endless deep jungle where nature is king – and the Guajajara Guardians want to keep it that way.

It's hard to understand just how big the Amazon rainforest is. As the largest tropical rainforest in the world, it sprawls across nine different South American countries. It has millions of insect species, thousands of different birds and more types of plant than anywhere else on Earth. And, for as long as anyone can remember, it's also been home to humans. Hundreds of tribes still live in the Amazon and many of them lead very traditional lives.

But sadly, they're not the only people with an interest in the rainforest. Over the past fifty years, huge areas of jungle have been cut down for their wood, and to make space for farms, roads and houses. Hundreds of thousands of trees are still being chopped down every month, often illegally. This deforestation is bad news for wildlife, bad news for the planet – which needs as many trees as possible – and bad news for the people who live in the Amazon.

This is why the Guajajara Guardians exist. This group, also known as the Guardians of the Amazon, is made up of people from the Guajajara tribe in Brazil, in the north-east part of the rainforest. Long ago, their ancestors learned how to hunt and survive here. They understood the weather, the animals and the seasons. They knew which plants could help them and which were poisonous. Today the Guardians are fighting to protect their ancient jungle from being cut down and to stop other tribes in remote parts of the Amazon from being disturbed.

Without the help of the government, this is not an easy job. The Guardians often have to work alone, patrolling the forest to try and stop loggers from chopping down trees, and this can be very dangerous. The tribe face violence, and

THE AMAZON IS
AN ENDLESS DEEP JUNGLE
WHERE NATURE IS KING

one of their leaders, Paulo Paulino Guajajara, was killed on 1 November 2019. Their battle is tough, but the Guardians know that giving up is not an option.

Their work is not just about deforestation. They also look after a tribe called the Awá, who have been living alone in the jungle for many years. The Guardians worry that if the Awá have contact with the outside world, their way of life might be destroyed forever. Protecting the Amazon is complicated, but the Guajajara Guardians show us that, by caring about the forest, and bravely standing up for the people and wildlife that live there, it is possible to make a difference.

Their story is not an unusual one. Many similar struggles are taking place – not just in other parts of the Amazon but in rainforests across the world.

Wherever there are trees being destroyed and tribes being disturbed, there are people campaigning to protect them. One international organization, the Guardians of the Forest, has brought together communities from Central America, Indonesia, the Amazon and other parts of Brazil. Their hope is to keep the world's rainforests as healthy as possible.

The Amazon remains a miracle of nature. The sight of its tropical green jungle rolling out to the horizon is truly beautiful. Toucans soar over the treetops, sloths hang from the branches and jaguars prowl through the shadows. But deforestation here remains an enormous problem and, now more than ever, the forest desperately needs all the care and protection we can give it. The Guajajara Guardians, defenders of their home, understand this better than anybody.

PABLO GARCÍA BORBOROGLU

Penguins are incredible creatures. They can look rather comical, waddling around on short legs, but don't be fooled. These flightless birds are resourceful, strong and determined. They've adapted to life in some of the most extreme parts of the planet, and their flippers help to make them fantastic swimmers. They guard their eggs, dodge predators and spend almost half their lives at sea, where they arrow through the waves like dolphins.

When Pablo García Borboroglu was a toddler growing up in Argentina, his grandmother used to tell him tales of the southern land of Patagonia. She spoke about her trips there in the 1920s, and described a remarkable kind of bird that lived on the coast. Penguins, she told him, took great care of their chicks and swam for many miles each day to find food. The birds had made a great impression on Pablo's grandmother – and they impressed young Pablo too. For the little boy, it was the start of a lifelong fascination.

When Pablo was eighteen, he made his own trip to see a penguin colony in Patagonia. The sight amazed him. The penguins covered an area the size of 500 football pitches. The noise was almost overpowering, but he felt a special connection with the birds. At the age of nineteen he moved down to Patagonia, soon finding a job as a marine conservationist. That was more than thirty years ago and since then Pablo has dedicated his life to protecting the world's penguins.

It is vital work. Today, these handsome animals face new dangers. There are eighteen different penguin species in the world and more than half of them are under threat. When we think of penguins, we normally think of the birds that live down in icy Antarctica, but most of the world's penguins live elsewhere, in places that are far closer to humans. This brings its own worries.

When penguins have young chicks, the parents need to leave the nest and catch fish for them. This food needs to be in seas close by, so that the parents can swim back to their chicks quickly. But climate change, pollution and big fishing boats are affecting ocean life, which means that

THESE HANDSOME ANIMALS FACE NEW DANGERS

many penguins are having to swim further and further to find food. Sometimes the chicks are left alone for so long that they die.

In 2009, Pablo started an organization called the Global Penguin Society, which educates people about penguins, so that they can help these birds have a healthy natural environment to live and breed in. Within just a few years of being founded, the organization was doing amazing things, such as protecting the land around one colony, which helped it grow from just six nests to more than 1,800!

The Global Penguin Society has even partnered with Disney, to help make an online game called Club Penguin, which allowed its millions of players to donate virtual coins to help real penguins. It has

brought more than 6,000 schoolchildren to see the penguin colonies with their own eyes, not just in South America but in South Africa too. And best of all, it has helped to protect more than 32 million acres of land and sea!

The work of Pablo and his colleagues has benefited millions of penguins, as well as countless other sea creatures that share the same waters. Just as importantly, Pablo is now optimistic about the future, because he sees children learning about the natural world and becoming passionate about looking after it. For a man who now works in the same part of Patagonia that his grandmother visited almost a century ago, inspiring the next generation is the best possible hope.

AUTUMN PELTIER

They called her the Water Walker. Autumn Peltier's great-aunt Josephine was in her sixties when she began walking the shorelines of the Great Lakes of North America. By the time she finished her mammoth trek, this remarkable woman had covered more than 10,000 miles. Her aim was to draw the world's attention to something that every one of us needs: fresh drinking water.

Today, her young great-niece is continuing her tireless work. Autumn and her family are members of the indigenous Wiikwemkoong First Nation, who have lived on Canada's Manitoulin Island for hundreds of years. The island sits right in the middle of one of the five Great Lakes – beautiful Lake Huron – so Autumn and her ancestors have been surrounded by water for as long as anyone can remember.

Autumn was brought up to think of water as something precious, something to protect. Unfortunately, some North American lakes and rivers have become badly polluted by pipelines and other human interference, meaning that many indigenous groups now have no fresh drinking water. This is what inspired great-aunt Josephine to act – and this is what inspires Autumn too. Since the age of eight she has been speaking out about the importance of looking after the environment.

Her commitment to the cause is so great that in early 2019, at the age of just fourteen, she was chosen to become the Chief Water Commissioner for the Anishinabek Nation, which represents forty different indigenous groups around the region. Her job is to fight for fresh water for all of them, and to raise awareness of the dangers of water pollution. She has met politicians, spoken at international conferences and campaigned for better rights for indigenous people.

It is Autumn's mission to make sure future generations have clean drinking water. In September 2019, at the United Nations headquarters, she gave a warning to big businesses which were harming lakes and rivers. 'I've said it once, and I'll say it again,' the teenager told the audience, 'we can't eat money, or drink oil.' Today, women from the community still walk the shores of the lakes to raise awareness – and Autumn, too, is making sure great-aunt Josephine's battle is far from over.

WANGARI MAATHAI

The house was small, with a thatched roof and walls of mud. It sat in a village in the highlands of Kenya, encircled by rivers, mountains and green forests. In April 1940, a baby girl was born in the house. She grew up with a deep love of the land around her. The girl later moved far from her village, but she never lost that love. Over the next seventy years she would become one of the most influential African women of all time, winning prizes across the world for her conservation work. Her name was Wangari Maathai.

From an early age, her teachers saw that she had a bright curiosity about the natural world. She worked hard at school, performing so well that she won a scholarship, and with this she was able to

go to university in the United States. She might have been 8,000 miles away from home, but she kept on working, kept on learning.

After returning to Kenya, she carried on studying at university. In 1971, she earned a special kind of qualification called a doctorate. This was a truly incredible achievement: Wangari was the first woman in East Africa to be awarded one. And she wasn't stopping there. A few years later she became the first woman to be the head of a department at her university. She taught students about different animals and how to look after them.

But Wangari had bigger plans too. She was worried about the environment, and especially about the trees that were being cut down across Kenya to be used as timber and charcoal. She was also worried that many women in the country didn't have the chance to earn money. So she decided to try and change these things.

In 1977 she launched the Green Belt Movement, which encouraged women to grow seedlings and plant trees, paying them small sums of money in return, and

taught people that the best way to protect the land around them was to care for it themselves. It encouraged community work, defended forests and argued for fairer environmental laws from the country's leaders. Its first action was to plant seven trees in a park in Kenya's capital city, Nairobi – but this was just the beginning.

By 1986, the Green Belt Movement had expanded into other parts of Africa. This meant Wangari's ideas were making life better in other countries too. The organization educated people about conservation and caring for the environment, and continued to help women to earn a living and forests to thrive. Those first seven trees in Nairobi were the start of something huge: by 2004, the Green Belt Movement had planted around 30 million trees!

Wangari's work didn't end at tree-planting. She and her supporters angered the government in 1989 when they campaigned to stop a big tower block being built in a city park. Soon afterwards they also campaigned for greater democracy in Kenyan politics. More than once, Wangari was injured and sent to prison, but even when people tried to threaten her, she never stopped standing up for what she felt was right.

Wangari was now inspiring people not just across Africa but around the world too. She gave speeches at major international meetings, encouraging world leaders to think about conservation and human rights. She also wrote four powerful books. In honour of her work, in 2004 she was given the Nobel Peace Prize, one of the most important awards in the world. She was the first black African woman ever to win the award.

When Wangari died in 2011, at the age of seventy-one, memorial services were held for her on three different continents. Today the Green Belt Movement is still fighting for a greener future, protecting forests and giving hope to village communities. Wangari's story began in a simple house in the Kenyan countryside, and it grew into something that was heard around the world.

THOSE FIRST SEVEN
TREES IN NAIROBI WERE
THE START OF
SOMETHING HUGE

WENDI TAMARISKA

Morning is breaking in the Borneo jungle. On a branch in the tangled green depths of the rainforest, a baby orangutan crawls on to its mother. Its eyes are wide and round, staring out at the birds, trees and plants. The young animal uses its fingers and thumbs to tightly hold on to its mother's long orange hair, and together they start moving through the treetops. Within a few moments the two apes climb out of sight, becoming what orangutans always have been: a part of the jungle.

The word 'orangutan' means 'person of the forest', and these astonishing, intelligent creatures have been living here for hundreds of thousands of years. Growing up in a small village in Indonesian Borneo, surrounded by rainforest, Wendi Tamariska became familiar with their loud calls and the sound of them crashing through the trees. When he first saw them, he was amazed by how human they looked. But what he didn't know at that point was how much danger they were in.

THE WORD 'ORANGUTAN'
MEANS 'PERSON OF
THE FOREST'

Wendi studied hard, and when he was old enough to leave his village he moved to Samarinda, a big city in a different part of Indonesian Borneo, to become a teacher. Ten years later, when he came back to his family home, everything had changed. The forest around the village was gone. The trees had been cut down and the orangutans had disappeared. Before, the jungle had given his family fruit, fresh water and natural medicines. The ancient rainforest was a part of their identity. Now it was gone.

Wendi understood exactly what was happening. Here in Borneo, and across other parts of the country of Indonesia too, huge areas of rainforest were being destroyed to make space for palm-oil plantations and to provide wood for loggers. But when Wendi saw with his own eyes the damage this was doing – to the people as well as to the wildlife – he knew that it was time for him to act.

In 2010, he joined the Gunung Palung Orangutan Conservation Program, a project which looks after orangutans and other wildlife by protecting the rainforest and helping local communities. But Wendi quickly realized that this was not an easy

task. He saw that it was very difficult for people in small villages to have their voices heard by the government. He also saw how much power and influence palm-oil companies had. If he wanted to keep the rainforest as safe as possible, he needed to find a way to change this.

His idea was a simple one. He read everything he could about conservation, community engagement and government regulations. Then he talked to people. He spoke with the villagers and tried to understand their hopes and fears. He spoke with local government officials and explained why it was so important to care for the rainforest. This jungle, he told them, was one of the oldest on the planet, providing a home for orangutans, gibbons, sun bears, hornbills and all sorts of other incredible wildlife. He spoke so passionately and sensibly that before long government officials started visiting the villages themselves, to listen to what the villagers had to say.

Many years later, Wendi still does the same work. Sometimes, interference by the palm-oil companies makes his job difficult but, because he has earned the trust of so many people, Wendi is able to make a difference. He has persuaded many local loggers to stop their work by helping them earn money in other ways: they sell handicrafts to shops and grow organic food for local restaurants.

Wendi's calm approach to tackling a very difficult problem has been good news for the forests of Borneo. His hard work has meant that villagers and local government officials can talk openly to each other, and his aim is now to help as many rainforest communities as he can. Above all, he recognizes that the jungle is something to be cherished – and that its most famous residents, the wild and wonderful orangutans, need all the protection we can give them.

LEN PETERS

It is after midnight. On a silent, starlit beach on the Caribbean island of Trinidad, a female leatherback turtle emerges from the sea. She weighs the same as ten grown women and her inky-blue shell is wide and strong. She moves slowly up the sand in the darkness, using her long front flippers to haul her heavy body away from the waves.

The turtle is doing what her ancestors have done for millions of years: finding a safe spot to dig a nest and lay her eggs. If all goes well, two months from now her tiny baby leatherbacks will wriggle out of the eggs and flip-flap their way down to the sea. This mother-to-be faces all sorts of dangers – but tonight there's someone nearby to protect her.

Further along the shore, the red light of a head torch gleams in the night. It belongs to Len Peters, a local man who acts as a kind of bodyguard to the turtles. Of the seven species of sea turtle in the world, none are as big or as ancient as the leatherback. But these magnificent creatures are at risk. For many years people have hunted them, on shore and in the sea, killing them for their meat and stealing their eggs. Their numbers around the world have fallen drastically.

As a young boy, Len lived in a village where it was normal to buy and sell turtle meat. It was only when he grew up, and learned just how badly the giant animals were suffering, that he started to look at the situation differently. He soon decided that he wanted to do something about it. If the species was in trouble, there had to be a way to help.

So in the early 1990s, Len and a small number of other locals began patrolling the beaches at night, making sure the turtles and their eggs weren't being attacked or disturbed by people. This was often dangerous. Len was sworn at, had things thrown at him and was even wrestled by someone holding a machete. All this made him realize that his patrols weren't just important – they were vital.

They were also a source of inspiration to other wildlife-loving locals. As the years went by, more and more islanders became involved in looking after the turtles. By 2006 there was so much interest in helping them

that five communities around Trinidad came together, led by Len, to form a group called the Turtle Village Trust. Today, the group still protects tens of thousands of turtle nests every single year.

People's attitude to leatherback turtles has changed dramatically since Len was a young man. Rather than viewing them as meat, most people see them as creatures to be treasured. Visitors from across the world now come to the island to see the turtles, marvelling at the size of the females and the determination of the newly hatched babies.

The work done by Len and his colleagues has never been more important. When

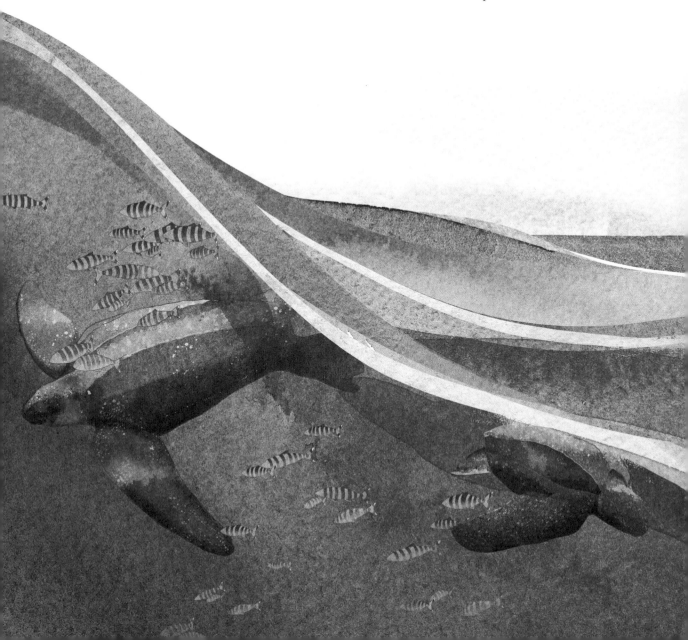

female leatherbacks arrive in Trinidad each spring to lay their eggs, every one of them has travelled an epic distance across the Atlantic Ocean to get there. No one knows exactly how they're able to find their way back to the same beaches, year after year, but they do. They are a true wonder of nature and we need to keep them safe.

The sight of a female leatherback turtle inching her way up the sand is utterly extraordinary. And, by following Len's example, the people of Trinidad can help to ensure that these super-sized reptiles have the future they deserve.

GRETA THUNBERG

Her teacher called out her name on the register, but no answer came. On Monday 20 August 2018, when she was meant to be at school, a softly spoken fifteen-year-old girl instead spent the day sitting alone on the cobblestones outside the Swedish parliament building in Stockholm. She carried a hand-painted sign that read SCHOOL STRIKE FOR THE CLIMATE. She came back to the same spot every day for three weeks. Within hours, her story appeared on social media. Within days, other people had come to join her, and the national newspapers were reporting on the strike. Within months, her name was known around the world.

Greta Thunberg was born and grew up in Stockholm, Sweden's capital city, together with her little sister, Beata. Her father was an actor and her mother an opera singer, but Greta was a quiet girl. She first heard about climate change when she was around eight years old and even at that young age she was confused: why weren't people doing more to stop it? If the future health of the world was at risk, she reasoned, surely we should all be doing everything in our power to help it.

This thought, and others like it, troubled her. As she grew older, she became anxious and depressed. Within a few years doctors had diagnosed a condition called Asperger syndrome. People with Asperger syndrome can struggle to be chatty and sociable, but they also find it impossible to ignore things they think are important. Greta has said that having Asperger syndrome is her 'superpower', because she feels it allows her to see things clearly and stick to her principles.

It certainly helped her to convince her parents about the facts of climate change. She spent hours showing them graphs, pictures and films to demonstrate how serious the problem was. Eventually they realized the importance of what she was saying. And that's when Greta knew she could make a difference.

When the story of an unknown schoolgirl sitting outside a parliament building reached the media in August 2018, no one could have imagined the impact it would have. Greta's simple protest drew so much attention that, at the end of those three weeks, she decided to return to the same spot every Friday, to continue campaigning against the lack of action on climate change. When other young people around the world saw what she was doing and decided to act too, this

A RACE WE MUST WIN
CLIMATE ACTION NOW!

movement became known as Fridays for Future.

It spread at an astonishing speed, so that by November, thousands of children in Australia were skipping school to support the movement. By December, there were protests in more than 270 towns and cities around the world, from Canada to the UK and from Germany to Japan. And on Friday 15 March the following year, just seven months after Greta had sat alone with her hand-painted sign, an estimated 1.4 million schoolchildren took part in a global climate strike. Greta had inspired people around the planet.

The incredible growth of the Fridays for Future movement made Greta extremely famous. For such a naturally shy girl, this could have been very difficult – but it also gave her a sense of purpose. She realized that she now had an audience of millions of people to persuade about the dangers of climate change. This was not the

time to stop what she was doing. Instead, it was just the beginning.

She began speaking at important events around Europe, meeting politicians, world leaders, other youth activists and even the Pope. Her commitment was so remarkable – a small Swedish schoolgirl fighting for a better world – that she was nominated for the Nobel Peace Prize, one of the most important awards in the world.

In August 2019, she travelled to the USA to attend a series of crucial climate events. She refused to fly – planes release harmful greenhouse gases, which are a major cause of climate change – so she spent two weeks crossing the Atlantic by boat. Her aim was to set an example to other people and, whatever she does over the years ahead, this spirit and dedication will surely stay the same. 'The world is waking up, and we are the change,' she said onstage in New York, looking out at a packed crowd. 'Continue, and never give up.'

FRIDAYS FOR FUTURE

Over six million. That's how many people joined protests around the world in a single week in September 2019, to show how angry they were about the climate crisis. In India, they marched through the streets. In New Zealand, they delivered a letter to the government asking them to declare an emergency. In Brazil, they waved banners and chanted for hours on end. In more than 145 other countries, they came together to demand change, gathering an incredible six million people into one united action group.

It took the actions of a single schoolgirl to start the Fridays for Future movement, but just a year after Greta Thunberg's solo protest first appeared on the news, the movement had become something international, inspirational and huge. Today, striking from school on Fridays is just one part of its work. It has galvanized a worldwide campaign, and for the millions of young people who join in, the aim is always the same – to stand up and make a difference.

Greta is just one of countless schoolchildren and students who have supported the movement. In countries like Germany, Italy, the USA, Canada, Mexico, Turkey and Australia, young leaders have worked tirelessly to bring as many people as possible on to the streets to call for change. Lots of these leaders will not see their names in newspapers or on websites. Their dream is not to become famous but to protect the future of the planet.

One of the most important things about Fridays for Future is that it gives a voice to all schoolchildren, wherever they live. That includes you! Climate activism among young people is not a new thing, but Fridays for Future has helped to transform it from a distant cry into a mighty roar. All around the world, organizations working to combat climate change now have a young army behind them. The movement has never been so strong as it is today – and your voice is as important as anyone's.

BAYARJARGAL AGVAANTSEREN

People call them 'the ghosts of the mountains'. Snow leopards have spotted coats, padded paws and soft tails. They move silently through the mighty peaks of Central Asia, stealthy pale predators slinking across the hills. They can leap over ravines, scramble up slopes and bring down prey three times their size. The snow leopard is one of the most majestic animals on the planet . . . but it's also one of the rarest.

Experts think that there are between 4,500 and 7,000 snow leopards left in the wild. Like many creatures today, they face multiple dangers. Hunters want to trap them, goat herders want to kill them and mining companies want to move into their territories. This last problem is the

most serious of all. On the high plains of Mongolia, where up to 1,000 snow leopards roam the wilderness, the earth contains coal, copper, uranium and other valuable things. Mining companies want to make money by digging them up – but this intrusion would be a disaster for the leopards.

One remarkable woman has dedicated her life to making sure this doesn't happen. In 1997, Bayarjargal Agvaantseren was working as a language teacher in the Mongolian city of Erdenet. On her summer break she was asked to do some translation work for a biologist who was studying snow leopards. As she learned more about these unique creatures, and the threat to their survival, she understood something crucial: more had to be done to help them before it was too late.

She realized that, to protect the country's snow leopards, she needed the support of the remote communities living close to the animals. She had to make them see that the leopards were something precious, not something to be feared, or hunted. Local herders often shot at leopards to stop them eating their goats,

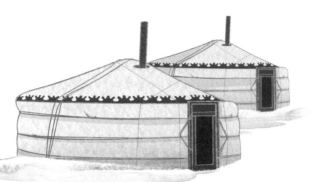

so Bayarjargal started a project that offered people money not to kill the leopards. Through the same project, local families could also earn a living by selling handicrafts. The idea was strong, simple and successful.

But bigger problems lay ahead. In 2009, Bayarjargal learned that large mining companies had been given permission to start work in the Tost Mountains, a wild region of Mongolia and a hugely important habitat for snow leopards. This was terrible news for the animals. Mining plays a big part in the country's economy, so it would be very hard for Bayarjargal to persuade the government to change its mind. But she had to try.

Through her years of work in the mountains she had the trust of the local herder families. They supported Bayarjargal's plan to stop the mining companies, but it would not be easy for her to convince the politicians. She began working with journalists and writing articles for the newspapers. She spoke with lawmakers, met with officials and helped launch a campaign on social media. None of this was easy, but she was determined to keep fighting.

It was worth every second of effort. In 2016, after years of dedication, she succeeded in getting a vast 1.8-million-acre area of the Tost Mountains protected as a nature reserve. Her plan had worked! By 2018, the mining companies had officially lost their permission to move into the area. For Bayarjargal, and the leopards living in this far-flung corner of the world, it was the best possible outcome.

Along with other determined conservationists based in Central Asia, Bayarjargal now works with the Snow Leopard Trust, which aims to keep the animals safe for decades to come. One of the most amazing things about Bayarjargal's story is that, in all her years of campaigning, she has never once managed to see a snow leopard with her own eyes. But she knows these masters of camouflage are out there, padding through canyons and across the high peaks – and that thought is enough. For now, the ghosts of the mountains have a future.

RIDHIMA PANDEY

Schoolgirl Ridhima Pandey lives in Haridwar, in the state of Uttarakhand, in northern India, close to the soaring snow-capped mountains of the Himalayas. Her mother's job is to help look after local forests and her father works for an environmental group, so from an early age Ridhima was fascinated by trees and animals. If she saw an injured dog or an abandoned kitten, she would bring it home and look after it.

But she also learned how dangerous nature could be. In 2013, when Ridhima was six years old, a terrible flood swept across Uttarakhand. It destroyed roads, bridges, woodland and houses, carrying away people and animals, and leaving some families homeless. For years afterwards, the young girl was upset and angry. She wanted to understand why it had happened, and what was being done to stop it happening again.

When her father explained that the flood was partly caused by climate change, and by the different building projects along the banks of the local rivers, she asked him to do something to help. Eventually he agreed to make a formal legal complaint claiming that the Indian government wasn't doing enough to help the environment. But because it had been Ridhima's idea, they decided that it should be her name on the complaint.

This is how, in 2017, the story of a nine-year-old girl taking the Indian government to court made newspaper headlines all over the world. India is the seventh-largest country on the planet, with a population of more than 1.3 billion, so for one young schoolgirl to be standing up against such a powerful government was extraordinary.

Several years later, Ridhima is still campaigning. She understands that the government must do more to protect the forests, clean up the rivers and stop damaging the land so that her generation will not suffer the consequences. And, by drawing international attention to such an important issue, Ridhima has shown us that no one is too young to be an activist.

ROSSANO ERCOLINI

Have you ever wondered what it would be like to be a primary school teacher? It takes a very special kind of person to stand up in front of a class and explain new topics and ideas. And sometimes being a teacher is a challenge. Having so many young children to look after is a big responsibility, and one teacher in Italy felt so strongly about protecting his pupils that he helped start an environmental campaign – which spread across Europe.

Rossano Ercolini lives in a small town called Capannori, in northern Italy. He was born there, grew up there, and later became a teacher at the local school. No one knew the town better than Rossano, so when a plan to build an incinerator – a large structure that burns all types of rubbish – was announced in 1994, he was worried. The fumes from the incinerator would harm the environment and make the air in the town bad to breathe, particularly for children.

He decided that the best solution would be to educate the whole town – not just about the dangers of incinerators but also about the benefits of recycling and composting rubbish, rather than tossing it in the bin. He spoke to the children and their parents, and then organized meetings in the town hall to share his ideas with everyone in the community.

This was a time when recycling was still quite an unusual idea. So when Rossano stood in front of his audience with a black bag, holding up old jam jars and banana skins, he was teaching people of all ages that different types of rubbish can be treated differently – and that rubbish isn't just something to chuck away and burn, but something that can be reused.

Rossano's argument was so strong that the plan for the incinerator was cancelled. But he didn't stop there. Soon his work helped inspire the Zero Waste movement, which spread all across Italy, banning incinerators and changing the way millions of people treat their rubbish. By 2019, the movement had reached more than twenty-five different European countries. Rossano still teaches at the same primary school, but his influence is being felt across the whole continent.

THE BLACK MAMBAS

When you watch a rhinoceros on the African savannah, with its heavy horns held low and its huge body armoured with thick skin, you might think its only worry is finding grass to eat. Sadly, this isn't the case. These magnificent animals are the victims of poaching, or illegal hunting, mainly because their horns can be sold for large sums of money. The problem is particularly bad in South Africa. Sometimes more than 1,200 rhinos have been killed there in a single year.

In 2013, a nature warden called Craig Spencer decided to do something about it. He set up a group called the Black Mambas, an anti-poaching team which works in Balule Nature Reserve, a large protected wildlife area in the north of the country. Two things make the Black Mambas unusual. First, they're almost all female, an approach which allows local young women to develop new skills. And second – despite the fact that they have to work in a reserve where wild animals and poachers roam – they're completely unarmed.

THE BLACK MAMBAS PROWL DAY AND NIGHT

The work they do is simple but effective. They patrol the reserve day and night, looking out for gaps in the fence, animal traps and any suspicious activities. They listen for gunshots, search for human tracks and check waterholes for poison. When they started, there were just six of them, but they now have a team of more than twenty. They understand that carrying guns isn't necessary if they do their job well. And, by being so visible in the nature reserve, they've cut the poaching by more than 75 per cent.

Rhinos aren't the only animals they're keeping safe. Poachers also target lions, elephants, antelopes and pangolins, and the Black Mamba's brave work is helping all these creatures. The team makes regular visits to local schools too, explaining to children how important it is to look after South Africa's wildlife. And, crucially, the rhinos of Balule Nature Reserve – the gentle giants of the savannah – can now wander the plains in safety.

RODRIGO MEDELLÍN

Do you have pets? A cat, perhaps, or a dog? Maybe a hamster? A rabbit? When Rodrigo Medellín was a boy growing up in Mexico, he also had pets – but not the kind that children normally have. They didn't purr, or bark, or hop around eating lettuce leaves. In fact, during the day they didn't do much at all. He kept them in his bathroom and every night he fed them cow's blood. They had sharp teeth, furry bodies and folded wings. They were vampire bats.

Rodrigo loves wildlife in all its forms, but he has been obsessed by bats for as long as he can remember. Many people are scared of them, so he sees it as his job to teach us how wonderful they are. We're lucky enough to have more than 1,300 species of bat across the planet and Rodrigo is committed to protecting as many of them as he can. In Mexico, they've given him a nickname: the Batman.

And, like the superhero of the same name, he doesn't give up. He has now worked in conservation for more than forty years, visiting caves and forests to look after threatened species like the lesser long-nosed bat. This bat performs a vital role in pollinating the spiky plants, called agave, that are used to produce the famous Mexican drink tequila. Thanks to Rodrigo, the population of these tiny flying mammals is growing.

But he isn't just batty about bats. He has also worked with jungle cats like jaguars and ocelots, travelling to wild places all over the world. Bats will always be his main passion though – and, amazingly, he hasn't just helped increase the number of bats in the night skies, he has also changed the way people in his home country think about them.

Rodrigo has taught at universities, won international awards and even had a film made about his conservation work. Sometimes we hear about people who make a huge difference to the natural world. The tireless Batman of Mexico – who still loves walking through dark, damp caves in search of his favourite creatures – is a shining example.

WILLIAM KAMKWAMBA

A curious mind can be a magical thing. When William Kamkwamba was a young boy growing up in a small village in Malawi, Africa, he always wanted to know how things worked. He was fascinated by lamps, batteries and wires, even though he didn't understand them. One day he even took apart his parents' radio because he thought there might be tiny people inside! As he got older, this curiosity turned into a love of learning – and it would change his future forever.

Life was not easy for William's family. Like most people in their village, they were farmers, growing crops not only to sell but also to feed themselves. William had six sisters, so his parents had to provide food for seven children. In 2001, when William was just thirteen, this became almost impossible. There had been no rain, and the crops couldn't grow properly. William's family, and many others like them, found themselves with very little money and very little food.

Soon afterwards, William started at high school, but his parents had no way of paying for his lessons,

A CURIOUS MIND CAN BE A MAGICAL THING

so he had to leave school. This was heartbreaking. But, as he looked at the dry fields around his village, he decided that he had the power to do something. He would go to the local library and use the books there to keep on studying. Then, when his parents had the money to send him to school again, he wouldn't be too far behind the other students. He didn't know it at the time, but the plan would have incredible results.

The library books William was most interested in were to do with physics. Most were written in English, which he couldn't read very well, so he used the pictures and diagrams to help him understand the words. There was one diagram that intrigued him. It showed a windmill, and as William found out more about it, he learned that its spinning blades could pump water and generate renewable electricity. Just imagine, he thought to himself, what my family could do with a windmill! Soon, a dream was born.

William was fourteen when he decided to try and build a windmill. He had no money for materials, so he visited the local junkyard to see what he could find there. His friends and family thought he was crazy. People laughed when they saw him picking out old

bits of metal and rubber from the rubbish. But slowly his dream started to take shape.

Anything that might prove useful, William kept. He found plastic pipes, rusty car parts and a fan from a tractor engine. He took a wheel and the frame from his father's old bike and gathered up used beer-bottle tops. He even chopped down a gum tree to make a tall wooden tower. But people were still puzzled by what he was trying to build. What was this strange boy doing?

Just a few months after William had first read about windmills, he was ready to try out his giant machine. Dozens of adults and children gathered round to watch as he climbed the tower. In his hand was a light bulb, connected to the windmill's motor. The wind blew. The plastic and bamboo blades started turning. The bulb flickered, died down again, then glowed brightly. William's windmill was working!

News of the remarkable home-made machine spread fast. When the newspapers found out about it, William was invited to speak at conferences overseas. He was able to continue studying too. Since then, he has made new, bigger windmills around the village, which pump water to the crops in the fields. He has helped improve life for his whole community in other ways too, using a solar-powered pump to provide drinking water and generating electricity for the school. In 2019, a film was made about his extraordinary story, *The Boy Who Harnessed the Wind*.

William's example shows us the power of determination and reminds us of the benefits that renewable energy can bring. And best of all? It gives us beautiful proof that scrap materials can be turned into something life-changing.

XIUHTEZCATL MARTINEZ

At the headquarters of the United Nations in New York, the audience fell quiet. A fifteen-year-old boy had just stepped onstage. He wore a smart suit and tie, and his long brown hair tumbled loose down his back. 'I learned from my father that all life is sacred,' he said, looking around the hall at officials from almost 200 different countries. 'He showed me that every living thing is connected. We all draw life from the same earth, and we all drink from the same waters.' The teenager might have been young, but his words were wise.

Xiuhtezcatl Martinez – his first name is pronounced Shoo-Tez-Caht – has lived an extraordinary life. Although he grew up in the USA, his ancestors were Mashika, or Aztecs, part of an ancient indigenous group from Mexico. Mashika people traditionally believe that humans are the caretakers of the planet so, even when he was very young, his family taught him about the beauty and value of nature. He first began speaking in public about the environment at the age of six.

His love of the world around him and his desire to make change happen have stayed strong. He continued to campaign throughout his teenage years, becoming the Youth Director of Earth Guardians – a group of artists, activists and musicians which trains and inspires young people to lead the fight against climate change. He has helped to get pesticides banned from local parks, campaigned to stop the spread of coal ash and even gone to court to try to stop the government from harming the environment.

But Xiuhtezcatl is far more than just a public speaker. In his late teens he began a career as a hip-hop artist and producer. At music festivals his songs get his message across to a brand-new audience. 'Can't let our differences divide us,' he rhymes in one song called 'Broken'. 'Gotta recognize that the change we want in the world has to start inside us.'

His passion for the environment has made him well known in the USA. In 2013, when Xiuhtezcatl was just thirteen, President Barack Obama gave him an award for community service and he

'WE ALL DRAW LIFE FROM THE SAME EARTH, AND WE ALL DRINK FROM THE SAME WATERS'

became the youngest of the twenty-four people on his national Youth Council. Two years later, he won a Peace First prize for his courage and commitment, and by the time he was seventeen he had received many more awards from around the globe.

Hip-hop music is sometimes seen as angry or violent, but Xiuhtezcatl has always believed that the best way to tackle problems is to find a peaceful solution. Through his music and his other activism, he recognizes that being optimistic and determined can be the most powerful response.

His heritage is also a vital part of what makes him so strong-minded. Across the planet, indigenous groups living

traditional lives are suffering from the effects of climate change. They often find it difficult to get their voices heard, but Xiuhtezcatl does everything he can to reach as many listeners as possible. In 2018, he performed fifty-five hip-hop shows around the world, touring for months at a time.

In many ways, Xiuhtezcatl is a normal American youth. He likes going to concerts and hanging out with his friends. But he is also a young man on a mission. He understands that we can't always trust politicians to do the right thing, so he keeps campaigning for a better, brighter future for the planet. Xiuhtezcatl describes himself as a 'climate warrior' – and he's not giving up the fight.

WENDY BOWMAN

It often takes courage to stand up for what you feel is right. One fearless woman, now in her eighties, has shown this more than most people. Wendy Bowman has been a farmer in Australia's Hunter Valley since the 1950s. The region is a handsome one, with rolling hills and fruit orchards, but it also has huge amounts of underground coal. Wendy's husband died more than thirty-five years ago, and ever since then she has battled to protect her farmland from big mining companies.

You might think that it would be difficult for one person to resist international corporations wanting to make money from the land. And you'd be right. In the 1980s, a coal mine near her farm polluted her water supply so badly that her crops died. Meanwhile coal dust from another mine blew all over her fields, so her cows couldn't eat the grass. She eventually had to move.

In 2005, she had to move again when yet another coal mine opened. She was given just six weeks to find somewhere else to live. By now she'd had enough. She settled on a small cattle farm in another part of the Hunter Valley, and when a big mining company told her it wanted to buy her land and open a new coal mine, she refused.

The mining company did not give up. They kept trying to persuade Wendy to move out, so she went to court to stop them. The court ruled that the mine could go ahead, but only if Wendy agreed to sell her land – and she was never going to let that happen. Even when the company offered her millions of dollars, she stood firm. She didn't want to see the countryside ruined and she didn't want to move.

In 2017, when Wendy was eighty-three, she was awarded the prestigious Goldman Environmental Prize for her resilience. Her story teaches us a valuable lesson of hope: that no matter how tough things get, protecting our planet is never something to give up on.

FRIENDS OF THE EARTH
INTERNATIONAL

On the outskirts of the Milky Way, floating slowly through space, there hangs a planet unlike any other. It has oceans, deserts, jungles and mountains. It has life that swims, life that soars and life that swings through the trees. It is a place of dazzling variety and infinite wonder – and it's the only world we've got.

Friends of the Earth International is one of the largest environmental organizations of all time. It was formed back in 1971, just a few years after people had seen the first colour photograph of Earth, taken from the moon. This view of the planet, a sphere drifting through a vast universe, inspired people to think differently about where we live. The world looked beautiful, but vulnerable too.

The first Friends of the Earth group was formed in the USA in 1969. Then, in 1971, the international organization came to life when environmental activists from the USA, the UK, Sweden and France arranged to meet in Roslagen, a coastal region of Sweden. Their aim was to set up an international group that would look after nature, fight pollution and campaign for a greener, healthier world. It was no coincidence that people from four different countries were there at the beginning. They realized that by working together and supporting each other they had a chance to make a real difference.

And they have. Friends of the Earth

International was soon living up to its name. By the late 1970s it was campaigning for the public to have a greater say in the protection of Antarctica. By the early 1980s it was raising awareness of dangerous pesticides, highlighting the threats to tropical forests, and putting pressure on countries that were dumping nuclear waste at sea. It tried to get as

many people as possible involved.

Fast-forward and the organization has groups in more than seventy countries, with a network of more than two million members and supporters. Rock stars, politicians, actors and royals have praised the work it does for the planet. The organization has become so important, in fact, that sometimes we take its work for granted – but its campaigns are vital.

The organization's many activists understand that change doesn't always come quickly. They have had to be patient, even when the issues they care about are urgent. For many years they have taught us how crucial it is to look after the world's bees, because the insects pollinate so many of the plants and crops we need. Friends of the Earth International campaigners have also encouraged more tree-planting, knowing how essential trees are to the future of the planet.

But nature and wildlife aren't the only things that the organization tries to

protect. It also works in countless ways to create a sustainable global society, from helping to provide solar-powered energy for families in rural Palestine, to advising people across the world to eat less meat and dairy.

Organizations such as Friends of the Earth International give people who are passionate about the environment a reason to be positive. They help turn millions of smaller voices into one strong chorus. When those first activists met in Sweden back in the early 1970s, they had little idea how influential their global organization would become. With the support of people from all over the world, however, it has grown into a movement that continues to make a difference.

The galaxy is a big, big place and we occupy just a tiny part of it. But only we can affect what happens to our planet, both now and in the future – and Friends of the Earth International is a fantastic example of people power.

MORE REBELS

MIRANDA WANG

What can you do with plastic that can't be recycled? This creative Canadian scientist found a way to reuse this kind of plastic, and stop it getting into the world's oceans. With her friend Jeanny Yao, she discovered a special bacterium that broke the plastic down into chemicals that could then be used for other things. Experts were so impressed that they gave Miranda a Young Champions of the Earth prize.

BHUTAN'S BIRTHDAY TREE PLANTERS

When a baby prince was born in 2016 in the mountain kingdom of Bhutan, he was given a very special present. Tens of thousands of local people went into the countryside and planted a total of 108,000 new trees in his honour! It's just one of many things that make Bhutan special. More than half the country is covered in trees, and it's also trying to become the world's first 100 per cent organic nation.

KYLE CATO

When he was a teenager, young South African Kyle Cato helped to collect two tons' worth of used bottle tops – about the same weight as two small cars! But as well as making his community a cleaner place, he also wanted to do something for the children at the local hospital, so he persuaded one local recycling company to buy them wheelchairs in exchange for all the bottle tops he'd collected. What a hero!

MAURICIO GONZÁLEZ-GORDON

This remarkable man was part Spanish and part Scottish. He became famous for making sherry but he was also a fiercely determined environmentalist. He loved birds, and in the 1950s he bravely stopped the ruler of Spain from destroying a very special area of woodland and marshes. Today this area is known as the Donana National Park, and it's home to deer, lynxes, wild boar and dozens of different bird species.

NIKITA SHULGA & SOPHIA-KHRYSTYNA BORYSIUK

Sometimes, a simple idea can make a big difference. Ukrainian schoolchildren Nikita Shulga and Sophia-Khrystyna Borysiuk were fed up with having so few trees in their neighbourhood, so they raised money for a composting machine, which turned food scraps from their school canteen into a lovely organic fertilizer for trees and plants. But things didn't stop there – before long, their clever idea meant that hundreds of other Ukrainian schools got their own composting machines.

JESSICA O. MATTHEWS

Having a kick-about with a football isn't just fun – it can also light up a room! Nigerian-American inventor Jessica O. Matthews was still at university when she made a football that generated its own electricity. Every time it was kicked, it helped to charge up the battery inside it. The ball had a special socket for a reading lamp, and for every thirty minutes of play, it could power the lamp for three hours.

SASKIA OZINGA

This Dutch campaigner spent nine years working for Friends of the Earth, then in 1995 she started an international organization called Fern, which works to protect forests and the people who depend on them. She believes that the best way to help the future of the world's forests is to involve the people who live in them.

THE FONGUE TRIPLETS

Here's proof that no one's too young to be a litter champion – these inspiring triplets were just six years old when they made headlines for their rubbish-collecting! Yimi, Waimi and Mbetmi Fongue, from Nottingham in the UK, started making regular visits to their local park with their parents, using special grabbers to pick up litter and making sure the park stayed clean and green.

FRANCIA MÁRQUEZ

When the lands around her home in Colombia was being dug up by illegal gold miners, Francia Márquez became angry. The miners were cutting down trees and polluting the rivers, so Francia persuaded eighty local women to march 350 miles with her to the capital city to complain. They walked for ten long days, and when they reached the city they spent three weeks protesting. And the best news? Their protest worked and the miners were stopped.

YUL CHOI

Back in the 1970s, Yul Choi was sentenced to six years in prison in his home country of South Korea, for standing up against the government. He spent his time in prison reading books about the environment, and when he left he set up a special organization to tackle pollution. Almost fifty years later, he is the leader of the Korean Federation for Environmental Movement, and is still committed to fighting for a greener, healthier world.

MOHAMMED REZWAN

Flooding is a big problem in Bangladesh, where heavy rainstorms can leave large parts of the country underwater. This makes things like going to school very difficult, but one man came up with a plan to make sure children could still carry on learning: he started using boats as classrooms! Mohammed Rezwan's brilliant idea was such a success that today Bangladesh also uses boats as floating libraries, health clinics and playgrounds.

JADEN ANTHONY

Comic books often feature heroes, and the Kid Brooklyn series is no different – although this is a comic story with an environmental twist. Created by New York schoolboy Jaden Anthony and his dad, Joe, it features Jaden and a group of his friends, who have been chosen by an alien to be the defenders of Planet Earth. They have to use their superpowers to stop the world's natural resources from being destroyed. Go for it, Kid Brooklyn!

ROK ROZMAN

Slovenian Rok Rozman loves the water. He was once an Olympic rower, and these days he spends his time trying to keep Europe's rivers healthy enough for other people to enjoy. In 2016, he started the annual Balkan Rivers Tour, which sees hundreds of kayakers paddling through south-east Europe, raising awareness about the dangers of dams. 'Nature conservation is anything but boring,' he says. 'It is true rock 'n' roll!'

AZZAM ALWASH

Azzam Alwash was born in Iraq, where as a young boy he loved visiting the country's nature-rich wetlands. Then he moved away for twenty-five years. When he came back, he was devastated to find that war and bad government had ruined the wetlands – they were dry, dusty and ugly. He set up an organization called Nature Iraq, and worked hard to bring water, plants and wildlife back to the wetlands.

EXTINCTION REBELLION

Since it began in London in late 2018, the Extinction Rebellion protest movement has spread across the globe, from South Africa to the Solomon Islands. Sometimes abbreviated to XR, its main aim is to persuade governments and world leaders to do more to stop the climate emergency. The movement has become a way for people to come together and have their voices heard. Its logo is an hourglass, to show that the time for change is running out.

YEVGENIYA CHIRIKOVA

Forests are precious, so when plans were announced to build a motorway through the heart of an ancient Russian forest near Moscow, Yevgeniya Chirikova realized she had to try and stop it. The mum of two and her supporters organized demonstrations and petitions, one of which got signed by 50,000 people. Her campaign was so effective that the Russian president decided to halt the plans because of their unpopularity.

*Of all the creatures that walk the earth,
one is more intelligent than any other.
Humans are incredible. You're incredible.*

You have the power to change things for the better. You have the power to bring hope to the future, to create a cleaner world, and to protect not just the human race but the magnificent lands, seas and animals that make our planet what it is. Like the people in this book, you too have the power to make a difference. So, what will you choose to do?

'THERE IS STILL
A WINDOW OF TIME WHEN,
IF WE ALL GET TOGETHER,
WE CAN START TO HEAL
THE HURT WE HAVE INFLICTED
ON MOTHER NATURE`

- DR JANE GOODALL, DBE

GLOSSARY

ACTIVIST: a person who works to achieve social or political change. An activist might work by themselves or as part of an organization with specific aims.

CEO: a chief executive officer. This person usually has the highest rank in a company.

COLONY: in biological terms, this means a group of animals that live together, or a group of plants that grow in the same place.

CONSERVATION: the protection of our natural environment.

DEFORESTATION: when the trees in an area are burned or cut down. Often the forest land is then used for farming, ranching or to build houses.

EXTINCT: no longer in existence (when referring to an animal or plant).

INCINERATOR: an enclosed container which is designed to burn waste at high temperatures.

NATIONAL PARK: an area of land that is protected by the government. Often an area of natural beauty, or historical or scientific interest, a national park is preserved for long-term protection and so people can visit.

PESTICIDE: a chemical used to destroy plants or small insects and animals that are harmful to farm produce.

POACHER: a person who illegally hunts birds, animals or fish.

TYPHOON: a violent tropical storm with very strong winds. A 'super typhoon' is a typhoon that reaches sustained windspeeds of at least 150mph.

URANIUM: a chemical element. Used mainly in producing nuclear energy, uranium is a heavy, radioactive metal.

For Clara, and young rebels everywhere - Ben Lerwill

PUFFIN BOOKS

UK | USA | Canada | Ireland | Australia
India | New Zealand | South Africa

Puffin Books is part of the Penguin Random House group of companies
whose addresses can be found at global.penguinrandomhouse.com.

www.penguin.co.uk   www.puffin.co.uk   www.ladybird.co.uk

Penguin
Random House
UK

First published 2020

001

Printed in Latvia

A CIP catalogue record for this book is available from the British Library

ISBN: 978–0–241–44042–1

All correspondence to:
Puffin Books, Penguin Random House Children's
One Embassy Gardens, New Union Square
5 Nine Elms Lane, London SW8 5DA

MIX
Paper from
responsible sources
FSC® C018179
FSC
www.fsc.org

Penguin Random House are committed to a
sustainable future for our business, our readers
and our planet. This book is made from 100%
Forest Stewardship Council® certified paper.